Changes in Nature

by Amy Leggett-Caldera

PEARSON

Glenview, Illinois • Boston, Massachusetts
Chandler, Arizona • Upper Saddle River, New Jersey

| spring | summer | fall | winter |

This tree changes in each of the four seasons.

Our Changing Seasons

In some parts of the world, the seasons change. In spring, birds sing and plants grow new leaves. In summer, the weather is warm. Animals are busy. In fall, leaves on some trees turn new colors and fall to the ground. In winter, snow covers the ground. Most plants do not grow then.

Some plants and animals *adapt* to live in places with different seasons. This means that they change each season so they can survive. The plants and animals need to change to live in the different kinds of weather.

---

seasons: four different times of the year when the weather changes in some parts of the world

survive: stay alive

Extend Language   **Plural Nouns**

Some nouns name more than one thing. For nouns that end in the letter *f,* we change the *f* to a *v* and add -*es.* For example, the plural of *life* is *lives.* Do you see a noun like this on this page?

Migration

Some birds migrate when cold weather comes. During migration, they go to warmer places where it is easier for them to find food and water. When the ground gets very cold in winter, it freezes. Birds cannot find worms to eat when the ground is frozen.

Some birds fly many miles to get to warmer places. One kind of bird flies for about 85 hours without stopping! Other animals migrate to warmer places too. Some bats, fish, whales, and butterflies migrate.

migrate: move to a new place

Canada geese migrate every year to warmer places.

Hibernation

Some animals do not migrate. They do not leave their homes when it gets cold. Instead, these animals hibernate. During hibernation, an animal sleeps. Its body slows down. This helps the animal need less food.

For example, arctic ground squirrels hibernate for seven to eight months! Can you imagine sleeping that long? The squirrels have to get ready for hibernation. They eat a lot during the summer and get very fat. Their bodies live on the fat during the months they are asleep.

---

hibernate: sleep deeply to save energy and survive in the winter

Arctic ground squirrels hibernate for more than half the year!

Many animals hibernate because the cold weather makes it hard for them to find food.

Why Do They Do It?

Some squirrels, bears, and birds are just a few animals that hibernate during the winter. They do this because it is hard for them to keep warm and find food in the cold weather.

Some of their food freezes in the cold weather. Other foods do not grow in the winter. Arctic ground squirrels eat plants that do not grow in the winter. Without food, an animal can die. Instead of dying, these animals change their bodies. When they sleep all winter, they can live with less food.

Plant and Animal Changes

Some animals do not hibernate or migrate. Their bodies change when the weather changes. In winter, reindeer grow thick coats of fur. This fur helps to keep the reindeer safe from the cold. Reindeer later shed this coat of fur to stay cooler in the summer.

Plants can also change when the weather changes. Just like hairs on your head, some plants make hair on their leaves. The hair keeps the plants warm in the cold weather. The hair protects a plant too. Bad things floating in the air cannot get to the plant's leaves.

---

shed: get rid of

Some animals, like reindeer, grow heavy winter coats of fur to keep them safe from the cold.

winter

summer

The sun helps plants make their own food.

Why Do Leaves Change Colors?

All plants need water, sunlight, and a special gas in the air to make chlorophyll (KLOR uh fil). Chlorophyll is a special chemical that makes the leaves on many trees look green. Plants use sunlight to turn water and the gas into sugar. The plant uses the sugar as food. Chlorophyll can store sunlight so that the plant can make enough food.

In the winter, the days get shorter, and there is less sunlight. There is not enough sunlight to make chlorophyll. With less chlorophyll, the leaves are no longer green. Instead, they turn beautiful colors, such as red, orange, yellow, and brown.

---

chemical: something that helps a process or reaction happen

Time Goes On

As the weather gets colder and the days get shorter, less sunlight gets to the leaves. Then they cannot make any more food. This tells the leaves that it is time to fall to the ground. The tree is ready for winter.

After winter, the weather warms again. The ice melts. The trees grow new, green leaves. Migrating animals come back home. Hibernating animals wake up and look for food after their long sleep. Animals shed the extra fur they grew. Everything wakes up in the new life of spring!

Animals and plants wake up and grow in springtime.

INFINITY

BY JULIE ELLIS

CONTENTS

WHAT IS INFINITY?

You have probably heard of the word "infinity." You may have even used it before. Maybe you stood on a beach wondering how many grains of sand were there. Have you ever looked up at the night sky and wondered what lay beyond the most distant star? Maybe you played a counting game with a friend once. When she said "a trillion," you thought you could win by saying "infinity." Is infinity a number? Is it a place you can reach? Can anything be beyond infinity?

Even though it would be very hard and time consuming to count the grains of sand on the beach, you'd eventually finish counting each one. Infinity isn't the biggest number you can count. Infinity isn't the farthest distance you can reach. The word "infinity" literally means "without end."

THE BEGINNINGS OF INFINITY

Don't worry if you do not fully grasp the meaning of infinity. People have been confused over the idea for thousands of years. A long time ago, around 1800 B.C., mathematicians in India started discussing the idea of infinity. They said that if you take away a part of infinity, you'd still be left with infinity. However, if you add something to infinity, you would also still have infinity. About a century later, other mathematicians in India talked about different types of infinity. One kind of infinity was a line that went forever in one direction. Yet, infinity could also be a line that went forever in both directions.

About the same time, in a different part of the world, the ancient Greeks also wondered about things that went on without end.

They didn't have a word for infinity, but they had the idea. A Greek **philosopher** named Zeno thought of a paradox, or a contradiction – something that seems both possible *and* impossible at the same time. Zeno imagined a person traveling from City A to City B. In order to get there, the person would have to travel ½ the distance first. Then, the person would have to travel ½ the remaining distance, or ¼, then half that distance again, ⅛, then again, 1/16, and so on and so on and so on. This halving sequence repeats itself forever. So, Zeno **hypothesized** that it's impossible to get from City A to City B. However, people always reached their destinations!

This paradox is based on the idea that no matter how small a **fraction** is, you can always divide it in half again. That means there will always be a small distance left to travel. Even though the distance between City A and City B is a **finite** number, Zeno argued that the journey is infinite.

According to Zeno's paradox, it should be impossible for a traveler to ever reach his or her destination. ▼

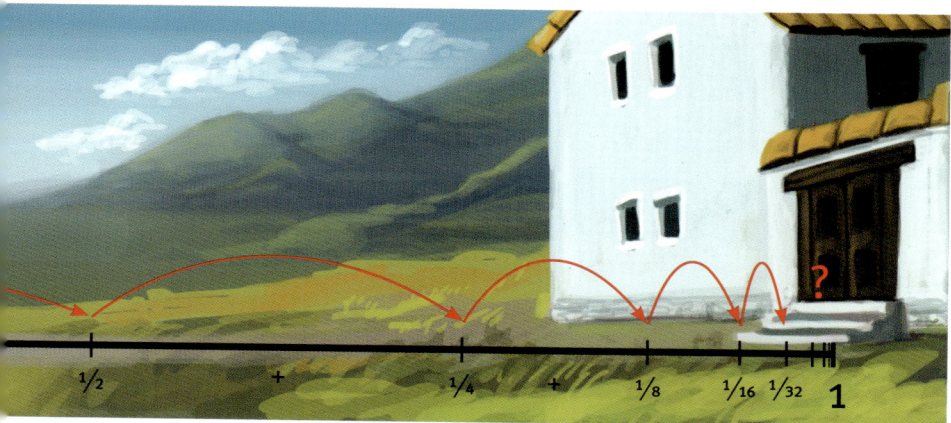

The word we use for infinity today comes from the Latin word "infinitas," which means "unbounded." Maybe you have seen a symbol used to represent the word?

The infinity shape is a special geometric loop. If you look at it, you can imagine moving around and around the figure without ever ending.

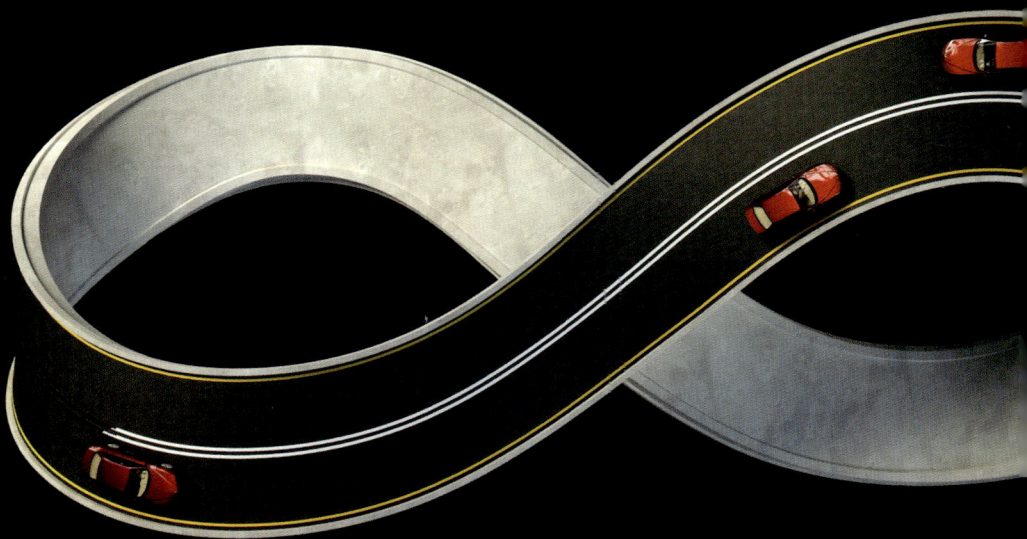

In 1655, a British mathematician named John Wallis chose this shape to stand for infinity. When describing flat surfaces, he used the symbol when he wrote, "I suppose any **plane** to be made up of an infinite number of **parallel lines.**"

◀ John Wallis

FAST FACT

You can test Wallis's idea yourself by taking a piece of paper and drawing two parallel lines. Keep drawing parallel lines across the paper. Do you think there will be a limit to the number you can draw? No. That's why the number of parallel lines found on any plane is infinite. Will there also be an infinite number of lines on a plane that aren't parallel? Yes.

INFINITY IN MATHEMATICS

What's the biggest number you can think of? One billion? One trillion? One billion trillion? A googol? A googol is a 1 followed by 100 zeroes:

$$(10^{100}) \; 10{,}000{,}000{,}000{,}000{,}000{,}000{,}000{,}000{,}000{,}000{,}$$
$$000{,}000{,}000{,}000{,}000{,}000{,}000{,}000{,}000{,}000{,}000{,}000{,}$$
$$000{,}000{,}000{,}000{,}000{,}000{,}000{,}000{,}000{,}000{,}000$$

If you counted all the basic **particles** in every part of the universe that we know about, you still wouldn't have counted up to a googol. Yet there's an even bigger number than a googol. A googolplex is a 1 followed by a googol of zeroes. A number that huge can't even be written down. Is it big enough to be infinite? No. Because there will always be a bigger one: googolplex + 1.

Hold that thought... perhaps there *can* be a number that has no end. It doesn't have to be a big number, either. In fact, it can be *less* than 1. A fraction can go on and on and on. Write the fraction ⅓ as a decimal. In order to do that, you must divide the 1 by 3. This is written down as 0.33333333333333333333333333333 33333333...

Mathematicians show this never-ending repetition by writing it as 0.3 (repeating). The 3's go on forever. Since the 3's will never stop, you could say that 0.3 (repeating) has an *infinite* number of 3's.

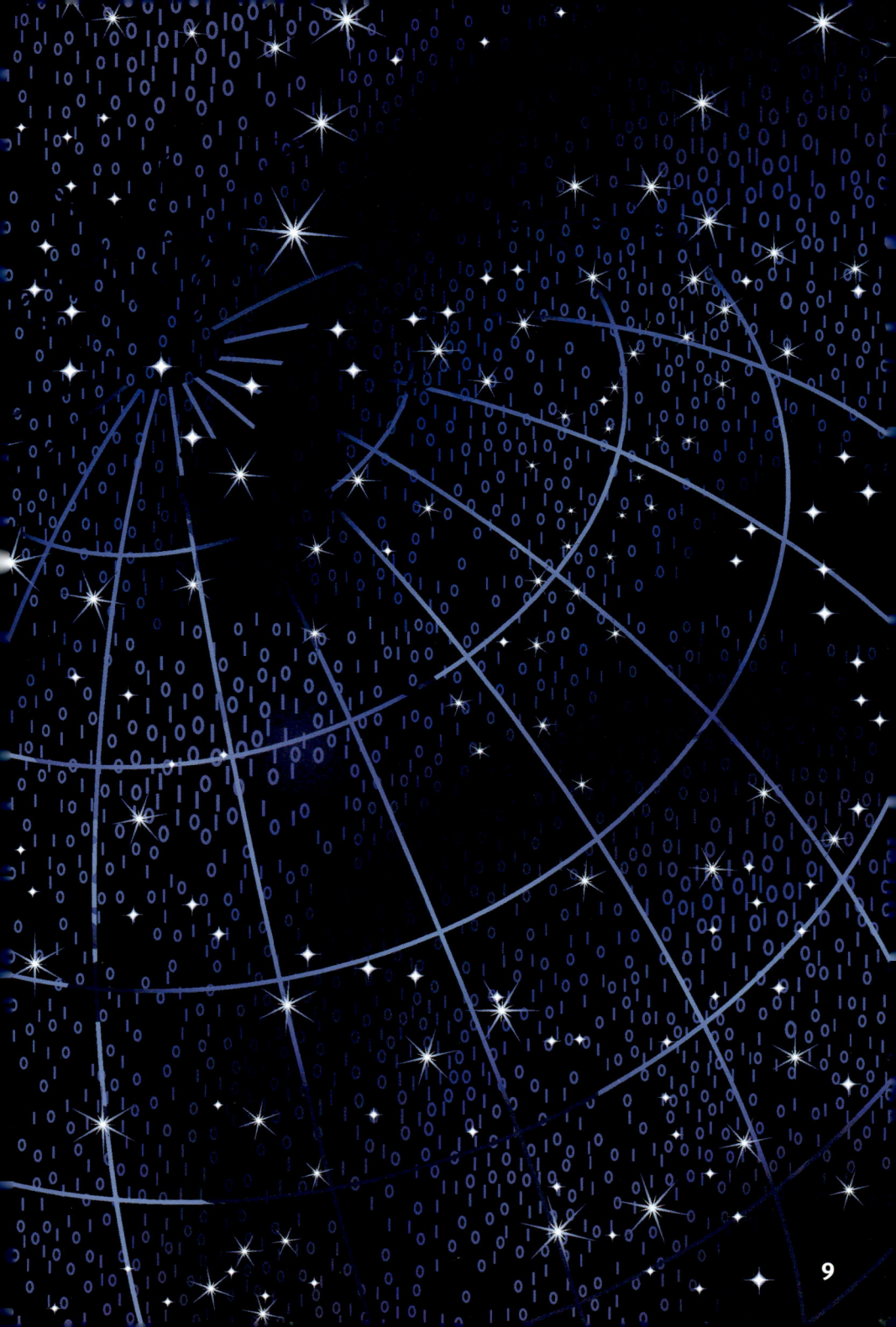

Can you think of another fraction that becomes an infinite number when it is written in decimal form? Well, $2/3$ as a decimal is 0.66666666666666666666666... or 0.6 (repeating). What about $7/8$? No. It is a finite decimal: $7/8 = 0.875$. The number ends at the five.

What you need to remember is that although some numbers go on forever, infinity itself is not a number. Infinity is an *idea*.

Despite it only being an idea, infinity is still used in mathematical problems. Remember the Indian mathematicians we mentioned in the last chapter? They figured out that if you add a number to infinity, you will get infinity.

$$\infty + 1 = \infty$$

If you subtract a number from infinity, you will still have infinity.

$$\infty - 1 = \infty$$

What happens if you multiply infinity by infinity?

$\infty \times \infty = \infty$ You will still have infinity!

What if you divide infinity by infinity?

$$\infty \div \infty = ?$$

A lot of people assume that the answer is 1.

It isn't, though. The answer is… well, we don't really know what the answer is.

(Yes, sometimes "I don't know" is the correct answer!)

We can't figure out the answer because we don't know the value of ∞.

Where else can we find the idea of infinity in mathematics? Look around you – you might be surprised. A Swedish mathematician named Niels von Koch once came up with the idea of inserting a triangle into a straight line. As each triangle is added, the line becomes longer. If we keep adding triangles, the line will go on forever.

Some people call these shapes fractals, which comes from a word meaning "broken."

When you look at the picture, does it remind you of something else? That's right. A snowflake. Coastlines, seashells, and peacock feathers are other examples of fractals that are found in nature. Can you think of any more?

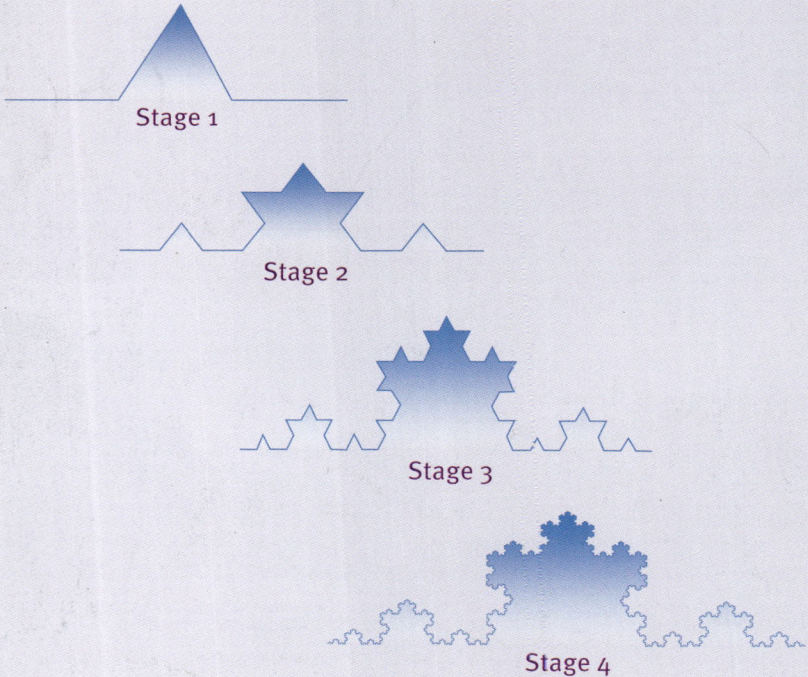

Stage 1

Stage 2

Stage 3

Stage 4

INFINITY IN SCIENCE

Mathematicians aren't the only people who think about infinity. Scientists do, too. **Astronomers** are often asked, is our universe infinite? This is a good question. It seems that every day, we are able to see farther and farther into **outer space**.

As we have learned with numbers, just being very far away doesn't mean the same thing as being an infinite distance away. In fact, you can assume that if astronomers can see a star in a distant **galaxy,** then that star is not an infinite distance away. That's because if we can see it, we know that its light has traveled to reach us. We know the speed that light travels is 186,000 miles (300,000 kilometers) per second. We can then calculate how far away the star is. That is a finite distance. What about beyond that star, though? As of today, we have seen things from distant galaxies over 14 billion light-years away. What about things that are farther away than that?

Astrophysicists often say they cannot answer that question. There is no proof that there is something out there, but there is no proof that there isn't, either. Scientists must base their theories on **evidence**.

There is evidence that the universe is expanding. The galaxies and everything in them are moving farther away. Yet that doesn't mean that the universe is infinite, either. That just means the distances between galaxies are getting bigger and bigger.

Now you know that infinity doesn't mean "very big." So, does infinity mean "very small"? When we divide ½ in half again and again and again, there is no end to the smaller fractions that we can make.

Scientists have found that everything is made of smaller and smaller particles. The diagram on the facing page demonstrates this. Look at the black-and-white molecule. Did you know that there are up to 20,000,000,000,000,000,000 (20 million, million, million) molecules in *just one grain of sand*? Now think: inside each molecule are atoms. Inside each atom is a nucleus. Inside each nucleus are protons. Inside each proton are quarks. Amazing!

This diagram shows the reduction in the size of particles from a molecule to a quark. The next big question is: what can be smaller than a quark?

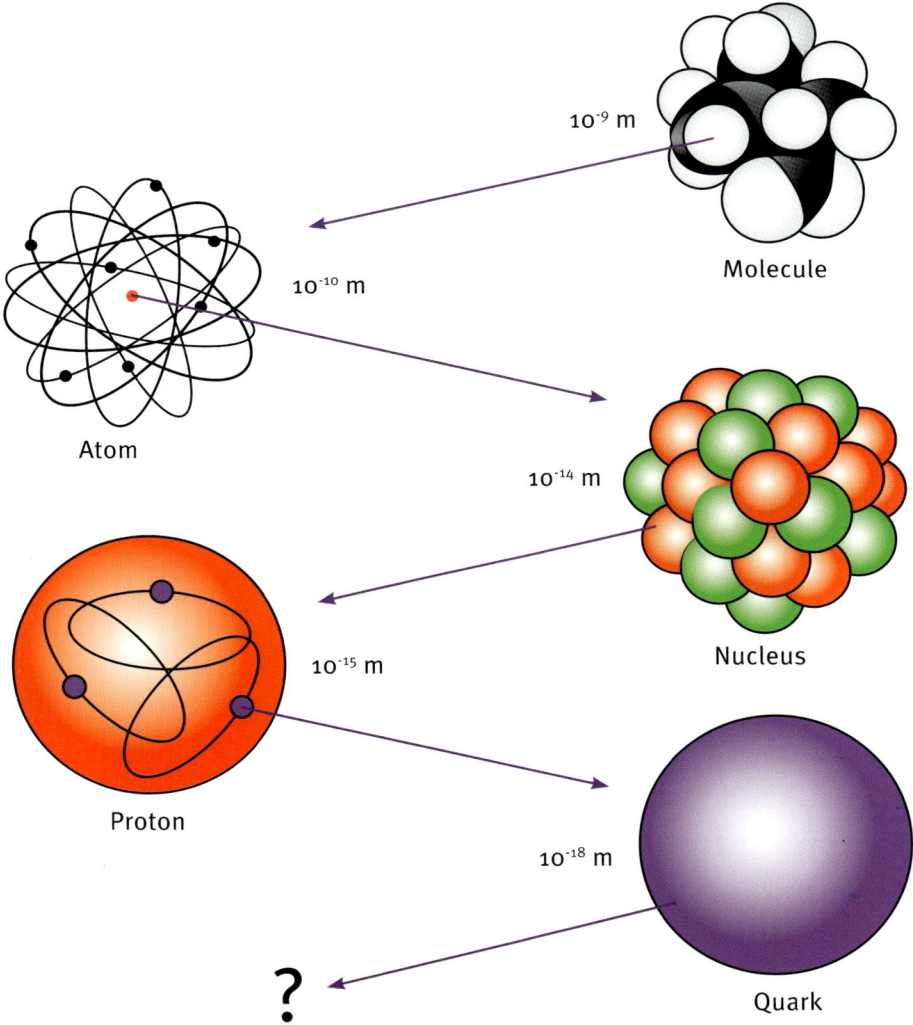

10^{-9} m

Molecule

10^{-10} m

Atom

10^{-14} m

Nucleus

10^{-15} m

Proton

10^{-18} m

Quark

?

Still, just because scientists continue to discover smaller and smaller particles, that doesn't mean that the size of those tiny particles is infinitely small. Once again, no one has ever seen any evidence to prove that this is true or not. However, many scientists do believe that there is a limit to how small these particles can become.

Maybe scientists won't keep finding smaller and smaller bits of matter, but just like numbers, the smallest particle can be divided again and again.

INFINITY IN ART

We have learned that infinity isn't exactly a number. It's an idea. We also know that infinity is difficult to understand. Sometimes art can help us understand theories by encouraging us to find new ways to think about them.

In 1802, the Romantic poet William Blake wrote a poem called "Auguries of Innocence." These are the first lines of the poem:

> To see a world in a grain of sand,
> And a heaven in a wild flower,
> Hold infinity in the palm of your hand
> And eternity in an hour.

What do you think these lines mean? How can we see a whole world in something as small as a grain of sand?

◄ William Blake

William Blake lived a long time before scientists discovered quarks. He didn't know that one grain of sand may hold over 100,000,000,000,000,000,000 quarks! So, we know he isn't talking about an actual world in the grain of sand. He couldn't really think that he could hold infinity in his hand. Likewise, eternity can't be an hour, because eternity means unending time – or infinity. Instead, Blake uses the idea of infinity to describe his wonder at the natural world. He suggests that a grain of sand and a flower are infinitely complex, despite their small size. By doing so, he challenges our way of thinking about scale and importance.

Let's look at another poem, this one by Jacob Bernoulli, a 17th-century mathematician:

Infinity
>Even as the finite encloses an infinite series
>And in the unlimited limits appear,
>So the soul of immensity dwells in minutia
>And in narrowest limits no limit in here.
>What joy to discern the minute in infinity!
>The vast to perceive in the small, what divinity!

Bernoulli also wants to find huge space in a small object. Maybe both poets want to remind us that infinity isn't only large, but that it is limitless.

Imagine that the infinity symbol, stretching into the distance, is like a series of fractions getting smaller and smaller, but never reaching a "finite" end point, such as "1". This is what Bernoulli means when he writes about something "finite" having an "infinite series" within it. ▶

Poets aren't the only people who try to express something about infinity. Many artists do as well. The Dutch artist M. C. Escher was very interested in mathematics and paradoxes in art. In drawings like this one called "Circle Limit III," he explored what some people called the logic of space. If you look closely, you can see how the fish connect to one another. As the figures get smaller and smaller, it seems as if they go on forever.

Even though you can see a circle's edge, you have to wonder if the images ever end. This is what Escher wanted you to think about.

These are just a few examples of how people have explored the idea of infinity. Maybe you can think of some others, or even make your own!

The artist's challenge was to capture infinity ▶ in an illustration, to give viewers a feeling of what infinity looks like.

UNDERSTANDING INFINITY

Now you know that there is a difference between being big and being infinite. The biggest number is still a number. It is a specific amount. Yet infinity can never be a number. It is a concept. Being infinite means being without limits. There is no limit to how many times something can be divided, and there is no limit to how far one can travel in a circle. There is no limit to how many lines can be drawn on a piece of paper, or how many points there are in a line.

To create an "infinity mirror," hold a mirror in front of your bathroom mirror and look at the reflection. Are you seeing infinity? ▼

People began wondering about infinity when there were still many unanswered questions in science. Today, we know a lot more than people living during 1800 B.C.

We now know that the speed of light is 186,000 miles (300,000 kilometers) per second. We have seen objects in the distant universe that are more than 14 billion light-years away. We know that matter contains particles that are only $\frac{1}{1,000,000,000,000,000,000}$ of a meter small. Our knowledge will keep increasing, but we will always need to leave space for those things that have no limits.

Mathematicians and scientists actually use "infinity" to solve problems about time and space.

Remember the ancient Greek philosopher Zeno, who traveled half the distance between two places and so could never get from City A to City B? Some scientists have that problem when they think about space. If you talk about space in separate parts, it is very hard to work with. When scientists do complicated calculations, they don't want to consider each separate point. They would rather think about all the points, or a continuous number, but since they don't know how many points that would be, they use the idea of infinity.

The same is true for anyone who is working with time. Between any two points in time, for example, between the time you got up this morning and the time you go to bed tonight, there will be a certain number of hours, minutes, and seconds. However, just like with distance, those units can be divided into smaller and smaller parts. You can continue dividing infinitely. (That isn't the reason why some days seem to last forever, though!)

It would be almost impossible for mathematicians and scientists to solve certain problems if they tried to use all of the possible parts. It is much easier for them to think of things as if they were continuous, or going on and on.

Remember that poets and artists wonder about infinity and create art that reflects their **musings**. Philosophers explore the idea of infinity, too. In fact, the different ways people can contemplate infinity are infinite!

GLOSSARY

astronomers – scientists who study the universe, including stars and planets

astrophysicists – people who study how objects in the universe interact

evidence (scientific) [3] – object or information that proves that something is true

exponent – tells us how many times the base is used as a factor. For example, in 10^3, "10" is the base, and "3" is the exponent.

finite – having an end or boundaries

fraction [2] – a quantity less than a whole, or less than one

galaxy – a large family of stars held together by gravity

hypothesized – formed a conclusion, based on an imagined situation

musings – creative thoughts

outer space [3] – the area of space beyond Earth's atmosphere

parallel lines [2] – lines that always stay the same distance apart and never touch each other

particles – small parts of matter

philosopher – a wise person, a deep thinker

plane – a flat surface

quark – a particle so small that scientists have never seen or been able to measure one

Academic Vocabulary Key	4	Economics	8	US History	12	Technology
1 English Language Arts	5	Civics	9	World History	13	General Arts
2 Mathematics	6	Geography	10	Health	14	Dance/Music
3 Science	7	General History	11	Physical Education	15	Theater/Visual Arts